GREEK BEASTS AND HEROES

The Monster
in the Maze

You can read the stories in the
Greek Beasts and Heroes series in any order.

If you'd like to read more about some of
the characters in this book, turn to pages 78 and 79
to find out which other books to try.

Atticus's journey began in
The Beasts in the Jar, and continues in …

GREEK BEASTS AND HEROES

The Monster in the Maze

LUCY COATS
Illustrated by Anthony Lewis

Orion
Children's Books

Text and illustrations first appeared in
Atticus the Storyteller's 100 Greek Myths
First published in Great Britain in 2002
by Orion Children's Books
This edition published in Great Britain in 2010
by Orion Children's Books
a division of the Orion Publishing Group Ltd
Orion House
5 Upper St Martin's Lane
London WC2H 9EA
An Hachette UK company

3 5 7 9 8 6 4 2

The Orion Publishing Group's policy is to use papers that are natural,
renewable and recyclable products and made from wood grown in sustainable
forests. The logging and manufacturing processes are expected to conform
to the environmental regulations of the country of origin.

A catalogue record for this book is available from the British Library

ISBN 978 1 4440 0067 2

Printed in China

www.orionbooks.co.uk
www.lucycoats.com

*For Mum, because she taught
me to love stories of all kinds.*
L. C.

For Beryl
A. L.

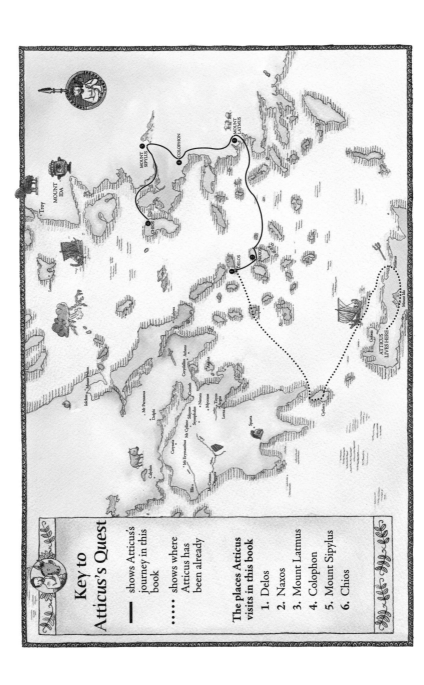

Key to Atticus's Quest

—— shows Atticus's journey in this book

······ shows where Atticus has been already

The places Atticus visits in this book

1. Delos
2. Naxos
3. Mount Latmus
4. Colophon
5. Mount Sipylus
6. Chios

Troy

MOUNT IDA

MOUNT SIPYLUS

COLOPHON

MOUNT LATMUS

CHIOS

DELOS

NAXOS

Seriphos

Lemnos

Cythera

Mount Ida

Miletus

Cydon

ATTICUS LIVES HERE

Iolchus   Mount Pelion

Mt Parnassus

Delphi

Corydallus Athens

Mt Cyllene

Corinth

Sicyon   Nemea

Symplegades   Mycenae

Lerna   Tiryns

Argos

Sparta

Cremmyo

Mt Erymanthus

Elis   Cronus   Olympia

Calydon

Contents

Stories from the Heavens

L ong ago, in ancient Greece, gods and goddesses, heroes and heroines lived together with fearful monsters and every kind of

fabulous beast that ever flew, or walked or swam. But little by little, as people began to build more villages and towns and cities, the gods and monsters disappeared into the secret places of the world and the heavens, so that they could have some peace.

  9

Before they
disappeared, the gods and
goddesses gave the gift of
storytelling to men and
women, so that nobody would ever forget
them. They ordered that there should be
a great storytelling festival once every
seven years on the slopes of Mount Ida,
near Troy, and that tellers of tales should
come from all over Greece and from
lands near and far to take part. Every

 seven years a beautiful
painted vase, filled to the
brim with gold, magically
appeared as a first prize,
and the winner was
honoured for the rest of his life by all
the people of Greece.

The Star of the Sea was waiting for Atticus and Melissa on the other side of Delos. It was crowded with passengers going to Naxos.

"Hello, Atticus," said Captain Nikos. "I told everyone about your tales, and they all wanted to come and hear the famous storyteller from Crete."

"Well," said Atticus. "Then I'll tell you about a nymph."

The Girl Who Grew into a Bay Tree

The river god Peneus raised himself out of the waters and leaned back on the bank. His long, green beard flowed down to his waist, and in his hand he held a wand of sweet flowering bulrush.

He smiled as he looked downstream to where his favourite daughter, Daphne, was washing her shiny green-gold hair.

He must remember to give her a gift, he thought, for only that morning he had found a posy of kingcups by his bed when he woke up. Daphne knew he loved kingcups. He dived underwater, and went to unlock his treasury.

Daphne was worried. The air was
calm and still, and it was a beautiful
summer's morning. But the swifts seemed
to be calling **"Danger! Danger!"** as
they screamed and wheeled across the
sky, and even the clouds of midges
seemed to be buzzing a warning.

 13

She muttered a prayer for protection to Mother Earth as she washed, and Mother Earth shivered comfortingly in reply.

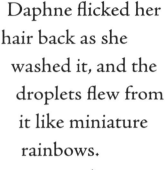

Daphne flicked her hair back as she washed it, and the droplets flew from it like miniature rainbows.

Just then a stranger stepped out from the trees near the bank and stretched out his hand to catch the water as it fell.

There was a small tinkling sound, and suddenly the stranger's hand was full of tiny jewels that flashed fire.

"For you, my beauty!" said the stranger, smiling and holding them out. "I am Apollo."

Daphne shrank back. She had never met anyone like this before, and she was frightened. He was so tall, and so golden, and he carried a bow and a quiver of arrows so bright that Daphne was blinded by their light.

She flung up an arm to cover her eyes, and as she did so, Apollo grabbed her around the waist, and threw her over his shoulder, laughing. He began to run into the woods.

Daphne screamed as she felt thorns and twigs catch in her long hair, and she kicked Apollo as hard as she could, and bit his hand, so that he dropped her with a cry of surprise.

 15

Daphne began to run. And as she ran she called out to Mother Earth.

"Help me! Save me!"

Mother Earth remembered Daphne's earlier prayer, and sent out her power.

Daphne felt her feet slow down, and as she watched …

 her toes sprouted roots,

her legs became smooth green bark,

and

 her arms and head became branches.

The hair on her head grew flat and smooth and pointed, and attached itself to the twigs sprouting out of her head.

 16

 17

A wonderful warm smell of spice came from the leaves. Daphne had turned into a bay tree.

Apollo was sorry for what he had done, and always wore a crown of bay leaves afterwards, so that he would never forget Daphne. But her father Peneus wept for seven long years at her loss, until his river kingdom flooded and burst its banks with grief.

Captain Nikos's boat lay far below in Naxos harbour as Atticus and Melissa puffed and panted their way over the mountains to the other side of the island, where they would find a boat to Caria.

"Oof!" said Atticus, sitting down on a rock. "What a twisty path – it reminds me of King Minos's labyrinth. Did you know that the only person who ever got out of that labyrinth alive landed on Naxos? I'll tell you about him."

The Monster in the Maze

The breeze brought the news. First it was a whisper in the trees, then it crept through the gates and blew against the palace windows.

"Theseus has returned!" it said.

At first the people did not believe it, for what good luck could come to a city that had been cursed for eighteen long years?

But then the palace trumpets blew, and the heralds went through the streets, and the people finally believed that King Aegeus's lost son had come back to them at last.

"Maybe he will stop the monster eating our children," they muttered to one another. "Maybe he is the hero we have been waiting for."

In the royal palace of Athens Theseus looked at the father he had only just found.

"You want me to sail to Crete and kill the Minotaur?" he asked. "But why?"

King Aegeus pulled at his long beard despairingly. "For eighteen years King Minos has demanded a terrible sacrifice from us. Every nine years we have to send

 21

seven girls and seven boys to be eaten up by his dreadful monster, the Minotaur, otherwise he will send his armies to kill us all. You are strong and clever. If you go with them, you may be able to think of some way of saving us."

Early next morning, a fleet of black-sailed ships set out for Crete.

"Goodbye, people of Athens!" shouted Theseus from the deck. "If I succeed, we will hoist white sails for our return. If the sails are still black, you will know I have failed."

When the ships reached Crete, the harbour walls were packed with faces as the thirteen children and Theseus landed. Each of them wore a garland of flowers as they were led towards King Minos's dungeons.

Theseus looked up, and standing
on a wall he saw the most lovely girl.
Their eyes met, and she smiled at him.
Theseus's heart pounded – he was
in love at once.

 23

The dungeons were dark and smelly, and that evening Theseus paced up and down as he tried to think of a plan. Suddenly, he heard a whisper.

"Psst!" it said. "Come to the window!"

"Quick! Help me up!" said Theseus to the boy next to him, and the boy pushed him up to the tiny barred opening, where he clung on tightly.

 24

Just outside stood the lovely girl!

"I am Ariadne, the king's daughter, and I've come to save you!"

Theseus was amazed. "But how?" he whispered back.

Ariadne handed him something through the window.

"I made Daedalus give me this. He's my father's inventor. It's magic string. It can never get tangled up. If you tie one end to your belt, and drop the ball as you go into the maze, you can find your way back by following the thread."

Then she handed him a sharp dagger.

"Kill the Minotaur with this, and when you come back I will be waiting with your friends and we can escape together. I hate my father for his cruelty, and I want to run away with you."

 25

Soon Theseus heard the clank of armour coming along the passage. He hid the magic string and the dagger in his vest.

"Now then, who's first?" asked a rough-looking soldier.

Theseus stepped forward. "Don't worry!" he said to the children, who were shivering and crying in a corner.

The soldier laughed cruelly as he dragged him through the deserted passages.

 26

"In there!" he said, pushing Theseus through a large iron door and slamming it shut.

There was a dreadful bellowing noise coming from somewhere inside, but Theseus quickly tied the string to his belt, dropped the ball, and walked forward. The thread unrolled behind him.

The labyrinth twisted and turned, so that Theseus became confused.

 27

The roaring got louder and louder, making the floor and walls shake, and soon he could hear words.

"Meat! Meat! Want man meat to eat!"

All at once, a monster burst round the corner. It had the body of a man and the head of a bull, and its jaws were dripping with red foam.

Theseus ran towards it with his dagger clenched in his teeth, swung himself up on its huge horns, and leaped onto its back.

The Minotaur bellowed again and tried to shake him off, but Theseus took his dagger and stabbed till it was dead. Then he followed the string back through the twists and turns of the maze to the great iron door. It was still closed.

"Let me out!" he whispered, knocking on it softly. And like a miracle, it opened.

There was Ariadne, standing with the thirteen children behind her. The rough soldier lay snoring on the floor, a cup of drugged wine by his side.

Quickly, they ran through the darkness to the waiting ships. The sails were soon up, and they were sailing away, safe at last!

As dawn rose, they landed on the island of Naxos. Theseus was just about to take Ariadne in his arms and kiss her when a shining ball of light appeared before them.

Out stepped the god Dionysius, and snatched Ariadne from Theseus.

"You may not marry her!" said the god. "For Zeus has written her name in the stars, and she is to be my queen!"

Theseus knew that gods are not to be argued with, so he bowed his head and walked sadly back to his ships. In fact he was so sad that he forgot to change the sails on the ships from black to white.

Every day, King Aegeus stood on the high cliffs of Sounion, watching for his son. When he saw the black sails on the horizon he gave a great wail of despair, and threw himself down into the sea below.

Although there was great rejoicing at the Minotaur's defeat, the people wept for their poor dead king. They named the sea in which he had drowned the Aegean in his honour.

Theseus became king and ruled Athens well for many long years. But he never saw Ariadne again. She married Dionysius, and in the end he made her very happy. And when she died, Zeus took her crown and hung it among the stars, so that her name should never be forgotten.

A storm rolled in from the sea as Atticus
and Melissa left the small port on the
other side of Naxos, boarding the big boat
that would take them all the way to Caria.

The huge waves and freezing rain
made Atticus feel seasick.

Melissa just rolled her eyes and brayed
mournfully.

"I know what, I'll tell you about
Philemon and Baucis," said Atticus.
"It might take our minds off the weather."
He pulled a rug over them both and began.

The Generous Couple

Zeus and Hermes used to stroll through the world, listening at doors and peeping into keyholes. They stood on market corners and hid behind pillars, and everywhere they went it was the same.

Cheating and lying, stealing and fighting – and even worse, murdering and killing for no reason at all. No one honoured the gods, and the temples were bare and untidy.

"What ungrateful creatures these humans are," said Zeus. "Let's wash them off the face of the earth and start again. I bet you a dragon's golden hoard that we can't find a single good human being before tomorrow morning, let alone two."

Now Hermes could never resist a bet, so Zeus and Hermes disguised themselves as beggars, and set off at once.

In the first village they came to they were pelted with rotten vegetables, in the next it was stones, and in the next they had the dogs turned loose on them.

It was the same all over the world. When they had finished running away, they found themselves at the top of a hill, in front of a tiny cottage.

 37

 38

Two old people, a man and a woman, were sitting outside in the sun, holding hands.

"Whatever has happened to you?" said the old woman, jumping up. "You poor creatures! Come and sit down while I get water and bandages for your cuts, and then I shall cook a nice big goose for your dinner. Why! You look half starved."

The old man went to help her as she bustled about, and soon Zeus and Hermes were sitting down to a wonderful feast, their cuts and bruises all bathed and soothed.

"What are your names?" asked Zeus, as he bit at a bone.

"I am Philemon," said the old man, "and this is my wife, Baucis."

As he finished speaking, the gods flew up from the table and revealed themselves in their shining robes.

"You are the only good people in all the world," said Hermes. "So you shall be saved when the great flood comes."

And so they were. Zeus sent a huge flood to destroy all the bad people, and the earth was covered in water for many weeks. Only one spot stood clear of the flood – a small green hill with a beautiful temple on it, and an old priest and priestess dressed in white.

Philemon and Baucis lived on happily for many years, and when they were very old, they asked the gods to let them die at exactly the same moment.

So Zeus turned Philemon into a sturdy oak tree, and Baucis into a graceful lime.

The two trees stood in front of the temple, their roots entwined and their leaves whispering to each other in the breeze. And it may be true that they stand there still.

It was cold and frosty, but Atticus and Melissa were glad to be on dry land after the long sea journey.

As they climbed past Mount Latmus they met a shepherd playing his flute.

"Will you give me some milk if I tell you a story?" asked Atticus.

The shepherd was delighted to sit down and listen to a story. "It's boring out here all day with just the sheep," he said. "Nothing exciting ever happens."

Atticus laughed. "I'll tell you a story about a young man just like you," he said. "And it took place on this very mountain."

The Man Who Loved the Moon

E ndymion the shepherd tapped his
fingers. Then he twirled his thumbs.
Then he counted the wrinkles on his
knuckles.

His flute was broken, his knife was
blunt, and he was **bored, bored,
bored** with sitting and looking at
sheep, sheep, sheep the whole day long.
His father, Zeus, was the ruler of all
the gods, and he was allowed to throw
thunderbolts and fight giants.

So why was it that the handsomest
young man in Caria was only allowed to
look after a flock of smelly animals?

At dusk, he set off home, driving the sheep in front of him. Their bells rang sweetly as they walked.

Just as he reached the top of the hill, he noticed a beautiful woman standing there. She had the full moon behind her, and she shone with a pearly light that lit up her long hair and her mysterious black eyes.

Endymion stared. "Who are you?" he whispered, falling to his knees.

The woman glided over and took his hands. Raising him up, she looked into his face and smiled.

"I am Selene, goddess of the Moon," she said. "And I will love you for ever."

Endymion forgot his sheep and his boredom; he forgot everything except Selene.

 45

She took him to a cave on Mount Latmus, and there they spent many hours together.

But Selene was not happy. She loved Endymion so much that she did not want him to grow old and die. So while he slept, she flew up to Zeus.

"Your son is so beautiful," she said. "Please enchant him so that he can never change, and I shall have him for ever!"

So Zeus went with her to the cave, and there he enchanted Endymion and put him into an eternal sleep.

Every night, Selene kissed him as she entered his dreams and in time they had fifty lovely daughters together, each more beautiful than the last.

Atticus and Melissa soon left Mount
Latmus behind and travelled up towards
Lydia. It suddenly seemed a long way
from home.

   Just outside the town of Colophon
they caught up with a procession walking
towards the crossroads.

   "Trivia and the children will be doing
this at home today," said Atticus sadly as
he watched the mayor and his wife lay a
pile of eggs and onions in the middle of
the road.

"We always give the goddess Hecate offerings of eggs and onions in the winter – perhaps she gathers them up and makes a feast for the gods."

Melissa flicked her ear crossly as a spider tickled her. It was trying to weave a web.

"That reminds me of a story about a spider. It happened hereabouts."

The Web Spinner

F lickety-thump, flickety-thump
went the loom, as Arachne tossed
the shuttle from side to side, singing
loudly as she wove. Her father had
invented a new dye that week, and she
smiled as she noticed how well the orange
pattern showed up on the cloth.

"Colour from carrots,
      Patterns from fleece,
Clever Arachne,
      Best weaver in Greece!"

she chanted boastfully.

Just then there was a knock on the door.

 49

An old woman was standing there.

"Excuse me, my dear," she croaked. "But I couldn't help overhearing your song. I'd always heard that the goddess Athene was the best weaver in Greece, but perhaps I'm wrong."

Arachne sniffed and tossed her curls. "Oh, Athene," she said scornfully. "I'm definitely better at weaving than her! Why, I'd beat her any day!"

The old woman began to grow taller and straighter. Her straggly grey hair turned silver and shining. An owl flew in and settled on her shoulder. It was Athene herself, and as she clicked her fingers, a magnificent silver loom appeared at her side.

Arachne's mouth dropped open, and the shuttle fell from her hand.

"I think we'd better have a little

 50

competition, my dear," said Athene, smiling dangerously. "And since you have so much respect for the gods, then perhaps that should be our subject. Time starts NOW!"

She turned to her loom and began weaving so quickly that her fingers flashed faster than fireflies.

 51

 52

 53

Arachne ripped the cloth off her loom, and set up new threads. Then she too began to weave. Soon wonderful tapestries started to appear on both looms.

Athene's showed Zeus and Hera, Aphrodite and Artemis, and all the gods and goddesses there were, dancing and feasting on Olympus. They were so realistic that you could almost hear their laughter and songs, and not a stitch was out of place.

Arachne's, on the other hand, showed all the gods and goddesses in ridiculous situations. Zeus was sitting in a puddle, Athene herself had sticky honey trickling down her face, Hermes was sitting backwards on a cow, sticking his tongue out at Hera.

When they had finished, Athene came over to inspect Arachne's work.

Not a stitch was missed, not a colour was wrong. But when Athene saw how Arachne had mocked her, she flew into a rage.

"Wretched girl!" she cried. "Since you think you're so good at weaving, you shall do it for ever more!"

As she said the words, Arachne's body shrank to a tiny ball, her legs and arms multiplied – and Arachne turned into a spider. She scurried up the wall and let herself down on a single thread of pure silver, looking sadly at Athene out of her many eyes.

And ever since then, she has been weaving and weaving and weaving.

But never again has she woven anything that mocked the gods and goddesses of Greece.

55

There was an old man sitting by the side of a well as Atticus and Melissa turned the corner on their way north to Mount Sipylus. His tall pointed cap had fallen over one eye, and he had a jar of wine beside him.

"Morning," said Atticus. "Any room for me there?"

The old man grunted. "Not from round here, are you?"

"No," said Atticus. "I'm from Crete. I'm looking for King Midas's palace."

"That ruin up the hill may be what you are looking for. Wasn't Midas the king with the donkey's ears?" said the old man.

"That's the one," said Atticus. "I'll tell you the story if you like."

The old man sat back to listen.

The Golden King and the Asses' Ears

Old Silenus the satyr was a bit wobbly. He'd had a party the night before with some nymphs and now his horns hurt and his hooves were tired, and he needed somewhere to sleep.

He noticed a nice comfortable looking flowerbed nearby, and settled himself down for a nap.

King Midas was counting his gold when he heard the commotion. Three guards appeared in the throne room, dragging Silenus between them.

"Found him in the garden, your Majesty," said the captain.

"Asleep in your best violets, your Majesty," said the corporal.

"All squashed they are now, your Majesty," said the private.

Now King Midas rather liked satyrs, so instead of punishing Silenus, he put him to bed and sent a message to the god Dionysius to come and collect him. As it happened, Silenus was a favourite of Dionysius's, so he offered King Midas a reward for his kindness.

"Whatever you like," said the god. "Just ask."

 58

King Midas had a passion for gold.
He was very rich, but he had never had
enough to satisfy him. "I want everything
I touch to turn to gold," he said.

"Are you quite sure?" asked Dionysius.
King Midas nodded.

"Very well then," said the god, waving
his hand.

As soon as Dionysius had left,
King Midas ran around the
room, touching everything.
Quite soon the room was
a-sparkle and a-gleam with
gold. The curtains, the chairs,
the table, the walls – everything was
made of gold.

"Hooray!" shouted King Midas.
"I'm rich!"

Just then, his servants came in to bring him his dinner. But as he grabbed a piece of roast goat to put in his mouth, there was a clang, and a bit of tooth dropped onto the table. The roast goat had turned to gold.

Quickly, Midas poured himself some wine. But as he put it to his lips, the liquid turned to solid gold too.

"Oh dear," said King Midas. "Now what shall I do?"

As he spoke, his little daughter ran in to say goodnight. The minute he had kissed her, he backed away in horror, for she had turned stiff and golden in an instant.

"NO!" he cried. "Dionysius, please, take this gift away!"

Dionysius stepped out from behind a pillar. "Tell me what is more precious," he asked. "A piece of bread or a lump of gold? A drink of water, or a golden cup? A child's smile, or a golden statue?"

Midas fell to his knees. "I never want to see gold again," he wept. "Tell me how I can get rid of it!"

"You must go to the river and bathe in it. Then you must pour river water over everything you have touched," said the god.

Midas ran to the river at once.

Oh, how glad he was when his daughter smiled and laughed as the water ran off her nightdress.

Oh, how happy he was to eat soggy goat's meat and drink watery wine. He vowed never to touch gold again, and he didn't.

But he did do one more stupid thing.

Pan the goat god had boasted that his pipes sounded better than Apollo's lyre, and they had agreed that King Midas was to be the judge.

Tootle-toot,

went Pan.

Plinkety-plink.

went Apollo.

Now Midas didn't want to offend either god, but Apollo was playing a golden lyre. Midas shuddered as he looked at it, because it reminded him of Dionysius's gift.

"Apollo's lyre sounds like a tinkling crystal stream," he said, "but Pan's pipes sound like the sweetest bird. I award the prize to Pan."

Of course Apollo was furious. "The man's an ass!" he shouted crossly. "And he shall have asses' ears to prove it!"

Right there and then large hairy ears sprouted from King Midas's head.

"What shall I do? Whatever shall I do?" he moaned, hiding his head in a curtain.

Luckily his queen was very clever, and she designed a special tall cap to cover his ears, so that no one would ever know.

The lords and ladies of the court thought the cap was very smart, so they all copied it.

Only King Midas's hairdresser was let into the secret, and he promised never to tell on pain of death. But over the years, the secret became heavier and heavier inside him until it was like a great lump of lead in his stomach.

"I've got to tell!" he groaned. "I've got to!"

So he dug a little hole by the river and whispered the secret into it.

But the wind carried the secret to the reeds, and the reeds rustled it to the birds, and soon the whole world knew that King Midas had asses' ears.

All his subjects laughed at him, but they all still wear the cap his wife invented to this very day.

Frost crunched underfoot as Atticus and Melissa picked their way up Mount Sipylus.

A small girl ran up to them. "I'll show you Niobe's weeping rock for a coin!" she squeaked.

Atticus sighed. He'd come here specially to see the rock, but he had no money.

"Will you show me if I tell you a story about Niobe instead?" he asked.

The girl's eyes brightened. "Yes!" she said. "Come on, it's this way."

The Queen Who Cried Rivers

Queen Niobe of Thebes looked at her seven handsome twin sons and her seven beautiful twin daughters playing in the palace courtyard.

"Surely they are the most wonderful children in the world, and I am the cleverest mother in the universe to have had them all," she boasted to her husband Amphion. "I'm better than a goddess at being a mother any day – after all, look at silly little Leto. She may have had one set of twins, but I've had seven! I think I should be a goddess too."

And she ordered the people of Thebes

 68

to put up statues of her in the temples
and worship her.

Now gods and goddesses have a
nasty way of hearing when humans boast,
and sure enough, a swallow flew up to
Olympus and told Leto what Niobe had
said and done.

Leto called her children Apollo and
Artemis to her at once. "Let us teach
this woman a lesson," she said.
"Let her daughters be frozen
to death by icy moonbeams,
and let her sons be roasted
by the rays of the sun."

Next morning, when Niobe went to wake her children, all she found in their beds were seven little blocks of ice, and seven little heaps of charcoal.

Niobe started to weep.

She wept so loud and so long that all the people of Thebes covered their ears to shut out the sound. She wept for seven long years, until the palace was swimming with salt and sadness.

Eventually Zeus himself became tired of her crying, and he took her away and turned her into a statue, and set her on the slopes of Mount Sipylus where her father Tantalus lived.

But even as a statue Niobe still wept, and the tears of her grief have fallen down the cliffs of the mountain in a great bubbling stream from that day to this.

Not far from Mount Sipylus they reached
the coast again. Atticus soon found a small
boat to take him and Melissa on the short
journey from Lydia over to the island of
Chios. As they sailed out of the bay the
eastern horizon slowly turned pink.

"Look!" Atticus whispered. "What a
perfect sunrise! Just the right time to tell
you the story of Eos the dawn goddess."

The Grasshopper Husband

Eos lived in a palace to the east of the east of the world. The walls were made of mother of pearl, and the doors of rose petals. The curtains were spun from cloud shadows, and the carpets woven from the softness of sky.

Early each morning, Eos got out of her bed and hung her huge fluffy pink pillows out of the window to be blown about by her sons, the winds.

Then she drew a bucket of dew from her magic well, and washed herself all over. The sparkling drops flew down to earth, to tell the world that day had come.

One afternoon, Eos woke from a nap in her garden and as she stepped out of her hammock, she looked down to earth and saw a most beautiful young man. His name was Prince Tithonus, and as soon as Eos saw him she knew she must have him for her husband.

She put on her best silver slippers and her best dress, and went to see Zeus.

"Well," said Zeus gruffly. "Marry him if you must, but don't come running to me for any more favours. Hera's not in a very good mood just now, and she wouldn't like it. I shall give him eternal life for a wedding present, and that will have to do."

So Eos married Tithonus, and they lived happily in Eos's palace without a care in the world. But although Zeus had

given Tithonus eternal life, he hadn't given him eternal youth, and soon Eos found a wrinkle on Tithonus's forehead, and then a grey hair on his temple. Tithonus was getting old.

"Oh my beloved husband!" cried Eos. "I shall go to Zeus at once, and get you made young again."

But Zeus was having another argument with Hera and would not see Eos.

 75

Weeping, she returned to Tithonus. Gradually, Tithonus got greyer and greyer, and more and more wrinkled. His back bent, and his legs curved, and he shrank and shrank and shrank until he was so tiny he had to be kept in a little basket in case he got lost.

His voice became small and shrill, and at last he turned into a tiny grasshopper, creaking his chirrupy song to his lovely wife for ever more.

Eos remained as young and beautiful as ever, but now the dew she sheds every morning is mixed with tears, as she mourns the loss of her handsome husband, Tithonus.

The story of the flood Zeus sent is called "The Greatest Flood" which you will find in *The Beasts in the Jar*. The 'beasts' in the title story are very different to the grasshopper husband!

Zeus turned the Generous Couple into trees growing side-by-side so they'd always be together. The gods were always turning people into things – can you guess what birds the Muses turned King Pierus's nine daughters into? Here's a clue: it's unlucky to see one of them but lucky to see two! Find the story in *The Harp of Death*.

Endymion was enchanted by the moon goddess so he would never change. Do you know how Odysseus got the better of Circe, the witch who punished his greedy sailors? Why not read "The Enchantress and the Pigs" in *The Sailor Snatchers* to find out.

 "The Robber's Bed" starts before the events in *The Monster in the Maze*, and tells the story of Theseus's birth and how he has to perform a mighty feat of strength to discover who his true father really is. But first he must get past horrible old Procrustes, the robber innkeeper with a very special bed. Read all about it in *The Dolphin's Message*.

Want to know more about Leto and her famous twins, Artemis and Apollo? Her story is in "Black Python and the Arrows of the Sun" which is in the book *The Magic Head*.